LETTERS FROM THE
SECRET PLACE

JEFF STRUSS

Elani
PUBLISHING

For information contact :
http://www.elanipublishing.com

Cover design by Peter Mitchell
ISBN: **978-0-578-60643-9**

First Edition: November 2019

CONTENTS

DEDICATION

This book is dedicated to my one and only: JoAnna.

You have supported me, challenged me,

and stood by me when no one else did.

I love you baby.

"It's gonna be worth it all."

ACKNOWLEDGEMENTS

Charles Stock: You showed me what it looked like for a pastor to be in love with God's Presence, and your cultivation of the church culture you created allowed JoAnna and I to grow up, to heal, and to go forth. I can't say thank you enough.

Josh McGready, Chris Pautrat, Abner Suarez: You guys have been true friends and you helped me grow up and get healthy in so many ways.

Grandma Struss: You prayed me into the Kingdom like you did so many others. Your prayer life and intimacy with Jesus is the greatest legacy anyone can leave on the earth. I know you are the happiest now in the Presence of your Savior. I'm doing my best to keep your legacy going. I'm forever grateful.

ENDORSEMENTS

Almost twenty years ago, Anne and I met Jeff and JoAnna. They were marked by hearts that burned to know God deeply. Through many seasons, we have seen that they radiate an inner fire of holy love. Opening this book to read, I found a treasure, multiple invitations to enter the secret place, to "taste and see" that the Lord is good. I was impacted by each "letter" that called me to go deeper into the endless love of Jesus. Read this book and find yourself more and more in love with the One who loved you from eternity.

Charles Stock
Senior Leader, Life Center Harrisburg, Pennsylvania

Encounters teach us and mark us. We all want more of them. Jeff brings us into his encounters in a way that brings the reality of them to the reader. Get ready for more passion and an expectation of what's possible out of the Secret Place.

Mary Baker,
Co-Senior Leader & Worship Arts Pastor
Zion Christian Fellowship, Powell, Ohio

Letters from the Secret Place is the testimony Jeff Struss' personal pursuit of God Himself that resulted in a lifestyle of life-changing encounters. His testimony is a simple invitation for you to forge your own personal history with God. This book is an invaluable tool and a must-read for every believer seeking to add fuel to their desire to know God. As you read you will receive:

- An impartation of grace to know God
- Faith to experience life-changing encounters
- Grace to stay the course no matter the obstacles you are currently facing

Abner Suarez, International Speaker and Author
For Such A Time As This, Inc.
Dunn, North Carolina

Many people have written books.

Fewer have written good books.

Fewer still, live what they write.

Jeff Struss has done all three in his inspiring, insightful, and personal work.

Anyone who reads this with an open heart will find themselves not only hungering for a closer relationship with God, but actually having encounters with Him.

Steve Espamer
Missionary Pastor
Connect The World

FOREWORD

People who say yes to Jesus are believers. People who continue to say yes when their yes is about to cost them are disciples. Disciples who have said a costly yes and teach others to do the same are my heroes. Jeff Struss is one of my heroes. His life and ministry have been a living invitation that has increased the volume on my own "yes" to the Lord. "There is a secret place where the Father hides us from the schemes of man, from the traps of the enemy, and He is drawing us all there."

I sat in a conference listening to Jeff Struss speak these words and I realized the power of an invitational life. An invitational life is vulnerable, sacrificed, surrendered, carries scars, and still says, "Yes." When you surrender to serve, you will get some scars. The secret place is where you take them. Saying yes to a journey into the secret place is not an invitation to a short visit. The secret place is not a timeshare. The secret place is not an escape from reality. The secret place is not far. Jeff Struss has built a life of faith there and invites you to dwell there too. He has peered beyond the veil and invites us to join him.

In these precious writings you'll find a seasoned minister of the Gospel taking you on a tour of your own journey with Christ from a perspective of hope and redemption. If you get the impression that Jeff has stepped into your soul, you won't be alone. It's an authentic prophetic grace that he carries, and the secret place he lives in is where the *authentic you* dwells. That's why his journey is so personal, and you'll easily identify. Consider this quote. "I want to create a heart posture that protects the reputation of God in my heart and mind. And one of the greatest enemies to that reality is when things don't go like I think they should."

Jeff has walked out a life of a faithful disciple, and in the face of highs and lows he and JoAnna continue to say yes. If you've been disappointed by life, ministry, people, and even feel let down by God, *Letters from the Secret Place* will encourage your heart, strengthen your faith, and turn up the volume on your YES! Accept the invitation and dwell in the secret place, and perhaps you'll be inspired to write letters of your own.

Bill Vanderbush

INTRODUCTION

Once again, I found myself shuffling around a Christian bookstore for hours. Often, I didn't even know what I was looking for. I just wanted "more". More of God. More of His Spirit and Presence in my life. More love and more power. (If you couldn't tell I was attending a Vineyard church at the time! LOL)

So as was my custom, I would walk into a Christian Bookstore and pray to myself, "Holy Spirit, lead me to the right book." What "the right book" even means is of serious question even as I write this, but apparently the Lord understood the cry of my heart and He would answer that prayer time and time again. However, this time would be different. It was near the turn of the Millennium and I was in a small bookstore outside the Baltimore Beltway. This would be the day that I picked up "The Practice of the Presence of God," by Brother Lawrence.

If you've never read that book, feel free to put this one down and buy it right away. It changed my life. It's a small book with short chapters.

There isn't a "point" except God and His Presence. It isn't dogmatic or exegetical. Rather it was created to draw the reader into encounter and experience with the living Presence of Christ.

Brother Lawrence lived his life stewarding the Presence of the Holy Spirit as his greatest treasure. Whether he was washing dishes in the kitchen or alone in his prayer closet, his attention to the Presence and his unceasing dialogue with God attracted the glory of God in his everyday life. People would travel far and wide to watch this man do the simplest of chores because of the abiding Presence.

He truly is our exceedingly great reward.

His book and life forever changed mine. Through the years I continually come back to it... To get refreshed, to get refocused. To dial into the "one thing". The "one thing" that David found in Psalm 27, the "one thing" that Mary found in Luke 10.

It's Him. He is our one thing. Knowing Him and being known by Him. It's the cry of Paul's heart in Philippians 3 and it is the explanation of eternal life given by our Lord in John 17:3. It's what was lost in the garden and found again on the cross. It's what we died to in Adam and what we have forever been made alive to in Christ.

Even now, my heart cries the cry of the prophet Hosea, "Let us press on to know Him."

There are a lot of incredible books available to us today. Books on theology, philosophy, practical ministry and more. This is not one of those books.

This book exists for the sole purpose of drawing you into an encounter with the Presence of Christ. That you would know Him. That your heart would long and thirst for Him. That you would seek Him and find Him when you search for Him with all your heart. The chapters have been written telling short stories that draws the heart to long for His Presence.

I found Brother Lawrence as a college freshman. Now, years later, as a pastor and ministry leader I can say with full assurance, there is no graduation from the school of knowing His Presence. There is no higher revelation. There is no loftier calling or destiny. To know Christ and to be known by Him, herein lies our call, and our success.

May the words found on the pages that follow draw you deeper. May the smell of incense found beyond the veil fill your soul and may the eternal flames of heaven burn ever brighter and hotter than before.

Let us press on to know Him.

Jeff Struss

HOW TO READ THIS BOOK

I titled this book, "Letters from the Secret Place," because I wanted to convey the nature of how the book was compiled.

Each chapter stands alone.

I chose to format the book this way in order to convey a unique reading experience. Rather than focusing on narrative, teaching, or chronology, the book is centered upon encounters.

Each encounter stands alone.

In fact, my prayer is that you would not be able to read a chapter without putting the book down and entering into your own secret place encounter there and then!

I did include reference points for the letters in order to convey a sense of context and background... these stories did not take place in a vacuum! Often what was happening in and around my life at the time had a massive impact on why a certain encounter took place as well as the end result of said encounter.

Perhaps in another book, I will thread together the overarching narrative of these encounters into a more cohesive and palatable story, but for now, please feel free to enjoy each chapter at a time. Allow the Holy Spirit to draw your heart into deeper and deeper places of love for Jesus, and let your faith rise that God has fresh and new encounters waiting for you in your own secret place!

Blessings and grace!

LETTER ONE

A SPIRIT OF WISDOM AND REVELATION

"…that the God of our Lord Jesus Christ, the Father of glory, may give to you a spirit of wisdom and of revelation in the knowledge of Him. I pray that the eyes of your heart may be enlightened" Eph. 1:17-18.

SOAKING. GAZING. PRAYING. BEHOLDING.

"Behold what manner of love the Father has bestowed upon us" (1 Jn. 3:1)

Spending time, long amounts of time gazing into the heart of the Lord and Savior.

I had been saved out of darkness, sin, and addiction and I had been thrust into His glorious light. Christ's Presence within was not merely an intellectual truth to be accepted, it was my life, my food and my drink. I was thrust into a season of seeking the Presence of the Lord through the word of God and through communion with the Holy Ghost.

Getting home from work or school I would shut my bedroom door and lay my bible in front of me. Putting my hands out as if I were to receive a gift I would say, "Lord I want to know you. Holy Spirit come and touch my heart." And He would come. Wave after wave of His fiery love would crash over my heart. One hour, two hours, three, four; however long He showed up was however long I stayed. It was the most life giving and fulfilling thing I had ever experienced, and I couldn't think of a reason not to stay and linger in this incredible liquid love of God.

His Presence would fill my heart and fill my room. I remember how one time I began praying standing up. Bad idea! I found myself losing my balance and falling backwards to the floor! No one had pushed me. No one had told me that was what I was supposed to do, it just happened. Another time I was praying, and a weird sensation began stirring in my belly. It began moving up my chest and suddenly burst out of my mouth in a language I did not know.

These were realities that were happening to me without anyone telling me it should be happening. It was the anointing of the Holy Ghost leading and guiding me.

"But you have an anointing from the Holy One, and you know all things" (1 Jn. 2:20)

"As for you, the anointing which you received from Him abides in you, and you have no need for anyone to teach you, but His anointing teaches you about all things, and is true and is not a lie, and just as it has taught you, you abide in Him" (1 Jn. 2:27).

"But the Helper, the Holy Spirit, whom the Father will send in My name, He will teach you all things, and bring to your remembrance all that I said to you" (Jn. 14:26).

One night I had gotten home from school and immediately went to my room. The Presence of God was so rich and so thick, I couldn't stop basking in His incredible love. Hour after hour passed and suddenly my alarm went off to wake up for school. I had spent the entire night in prayer and communion with my heavenly Father, my Creator and Maker. As I prepared for school that day, I was full of energy and excitement! I was shocked as I had simply lost track of the time.

During this time people in my school were getting saved, healed and set free. Several of these individuals were actually called into ministry and are serving the Lord as pastors to this very day. God was meeting me in the secret place, but what He was revealing to me in the secret place was spilling out into the public place.

As I spent more and more time in His Presence and in the Word, things began to happen which I had no grid for. He began speaking to me and showing me things. I would have dreams that spoke of my future and the call that He had on my life. As I yielded to the Holy Spirit and submitted myself to Him these encounters began to increase, and my heart was enlarged by our powerful and awesome God.

One night as I was deep in prayer, I began hearing a friend of mine praying for me. The odd part of this was that I was in Baltimore, Maryland. and they were in D.C., over thirty miles away! That night as I laid down in bed, I felt the sensation of being lifted out of my room. I was perplexed and frightened! I felt myself flying through the air and all the sensations were filling my being. I don't usually do very well with heights and the reality of flying through the air was genuinely frightening! I said, "No! No! No!". Immediately I changed directions and began flying back to my home and my bedroom. I saw myself lying there in bed and my spirit went back into my body. I flung up from the bed in fear. This experience happened again, and again; I told the Lord no!

Sometime before this encounter I had read that the famous revivalist of the First Great Awakening, Jonathan Edwards had prayed a prayer that went like this, "Burn eternity on my eyes." I understood that my revelation of the reality of Heaven would drastically change my engagement of earth and what I believed was possible with God. I took Jonathan Edwards prayer and made it my own: "God! Burn eternity on my eyes! Show me Heaven or show me Hell, I don't care. Just burn eternity on my eyes!"

"If then you were raised with Christ, seek those things which are above, where Christ is, sitting at the right hand of God. Set your mind on things above, not on things on the earth. For you died, and your life is hidden with Christ in God" (Col. 3:1-3)

I had prayed this prayer faithfully and now God was answering me, yet the fear of it all kept me rejecting what God wanted to do. I thought for sure I had ruined everything. What person is offered to go to Heaven by God and says no? I lamented my cowardice and fearfulness. I repented and cried out to the Lord.

A year passed.

I laid down to sleep one night only to find myself in the middle of a great expanse.

Christ spoke of this place in the parable of Lazarus and the rich man. In the parable, Abraham states to the rich man who is in hell, "between us and you there is a great chasm fixed, so that those who wish to come over from here to you will not be able, and that none may cross over from there to us" (Lk. 16:26). I found myself in that chasm suspended in air and I knew I was in the place between Heaven and Hell.

I had been praying for over a year, "Show me Heaven or show me Hell, just burn eternity on my eyes," and now I was suspended between these two locations and I heard the Lord speak to me, "You Choose."

I was struck with wonder! Choose?! In the split of a second I said, "I am going up!" Immediately I began flying through the air. I could feel the rush of the air against my skin as I flew into the atmosphere. I saw clouds pass by and then stars. All the universe began flying by me as I flew deeper and deeper into space. Off in the distance I saw something glowing. As came nearer the shape began to be clear. It was a city suspended in air. Large sapphire stones glowed around the foundation and I realized where I was: Zion, the heavenly Jerusalem.

As I sped faster and faster towards this city, I realized I was underneath it. I plowed right into the foundation of the city and surprisingly instead of being crushed I popped right through the foundation and found myself lying face down on an oriental carpet. I lifted my head slowly and began to look around.

I was in an office. In front of me was a beautiful bay window with padded cushions on the built-in bench with cupboards underneath. Light was pouring through the window and I knew it was beautiful outside. To my left was a globe that was beautiful and majestic. Bookcases lined the wall to my left and hardwood floor lay beneath the area rug I found myself on. Everything was real, everything was beautiful. It was as real as this computer that I am typing on right now. I stood up completely overwhelmed. Overwhelmed that I had just traveled through space and time. Overwhelmed at the heavenly city that was suspended in space, and overwhelmed by this gorgeous room I now found myself in.

Behind me was what I understood to be the backside of a row of bookcases that served as a divider in the room. I slowly walked around the bookcases to my right and as I did, I saw a beautiful wooden desk and behind that desk sat Jesus Christ reading the book of Jeremiah.

I can't begin to describe the flood of emotions that came over me in that moment beside saying that it is indescribable. I fell to my knees in worship and began trembling. I longed to look upon Him, but my trembling heart would barely allow it. With all the strength I could muster I raised one hand towards Him in worship and simply said, "You are so beautiful. You are so beautiful."

"My heart is overflowing with a good theme; I recite my composition concerning the King; My tongue is the pen of a ready writer. You are fairer than the sons of men; Grace is poured upon Your lips; therefore, God has blessed You forever" (Ps. 45:1-2)

"What is thy beloved more than another beloved, O thou fairest among women? what is thy beloved more than another beloved, that thou dost so charge us? My beloved is white and ruddy, the chiefest among ten thousand. His head is as the most fine gold, his locks are bushy, and black as a raven. His eyes are as the eyes of doves by the rivers of waters, washed with milk, and fitly set. His cheeks are as a bed of spices, as sweet flowers: his lips like lilies, dropping sweet smelling myrrh. His hands are as gold rings set with the beryl: his belly is as bright ivory overlaid with

sapphires. His legs are as pillars of marble, set upon sockets of fine gold: his countenance is as Lebanon, excellent as the cedars. His mouth is most sweet: yea, he is altogether lovely. This is my beloved, and this is my friend, O daughters of Jerusalem." Song 5:9-16.

My weakness and His strength. My dependency and His provision. My lowliness and His loftiness. All that I had read and I all that I perceived was true. I began to be washed in a revelation of the Lord and King Jesus Christ. He revealed Himself to me not as a lamb or as a conquering King. He revealed Himself to me as the Jewish man. Brown eyes, brown hair, a short brown beard and dark skin. I was not struck by his appearance but by the substance of who He really is: God in the flesh.

I don't know how long I knelt there worshipping Him. But after some time, He rose and walked to the right side of His desk. I felt that I was to rise as well. I found strength to get off of my knees and stand. I turned to walk around His desk and again bookcases lined the far wall all filled with books. There was also a built-in aquarium in this row of bookcases with fish in it that I don't believe are anywhere in the earth! I turned and looked at Him and He looked at me.

On the earth we can be thinking one thing but actually say another. We can have one thing going on inside of us but deceive those around us by saying something different. In Heaven this is not so. What is inside of you is apparent to all that are around you. There is not the need for language like there is here on the earth.

I stood there and gazed at Him and He gazed at me. Without a word spoken He communicated His deep love and affection for me. He shared with me His heart in a way that I cannot explain or communicate. It was a heavenly communion and a mingling of hearts. I felt His emotions towards me in waves. Just gazing upon Him was enough for me.

After some time had passed, He changed His posture and moved one leg backwards as if readying for a race. Suddenly He charged towards me and opened His arms. To my surprise He lowered His shoulder and wrapped His arms around me. Continuing to run forward He launched me into the air and in much of the same way that a linebacker would tackle a quarterback, He tackled me and drove me into the floor. But instead of feeling the pain of this event, when I hit the floor, I went right through it! I once again found myself underneath this heavenly city falling backwards into space! I once again saw the glowing sapphire stones and the city began to disappear into the distance.

I now turned to look downwards, and the entire event began in reverse! I saw the stars and space whirling by me at incredible speed. I saw clouds and the earth. I then saw my home and before I knew it, I plunged through my roof and into my bedroom and with breakneck speed landed inside my body. The force of my spirit hitting my body woke my wife up from sleep. I lay there trembling and unable to speak. Eventually I was able to mutter, "I think I just went to Heaven."

That event took place over 10 years ago. I wouldn't speak of it to anyone but my wife for several years. It was such an intimate gift that I felt was just for me. Only through time and more prayer did the Lord begin to let me share some of this story with others. As I have traveled the country and shared this story, it has often resulted in others who are listening in the congregation being thrust into their own encounters. Individuals often report seeing heaven, or angels or being taken to Heaven and even Hell. One night as I shared on supernatural encounters like this a burning smell filled the entire room. Everyone smelt it.

That night a young man was taken to Hell and shown the torment of those who have entered eternity apart from Christ. He was trembling with fear and trepidation and could not speak for some time after that encounter.

All throughout the Bible, God has taken people into prophetic encounters to show them His heart, His plan, and His will. He has pulled back the veil in order to impress upon mankind the reality of His Kingdom. My prayer for you is the same as the prayer of the apostle Paul: That the Lord Jesus would give to you a spirit of wisdom and revelation in the knowledge of Him; that your eyes would be open to receive and understand all that God has for you in Him.

LETTER TWO

THE FIRE OF REJECTION

"Then the mother of the sons of Zebedee came to Jesus with her sons, bowing down and making a request of Him. And He said to her, "What do you wish?" She said to Him, "Command that in Your kingdom these two sons of mine may sit one on Your right and one on Your left." But Jesus answered, "You do not know what you are asking. Are you able to drink the cup that I am about to drink?" They said to Him, "We are able." He said to them, "My cup you shall drink; but to sit on My right and on My left, this is not Mine to give, but it is for those for whom it has been prepared by My Father" *Matt. 20:20-23.*

IT IS A MIXED CUP. THIS FELLOWSHIP, THIS NEARNESS TO CHRIST. HOW CLOSE AND HOW NEAR DO YOU WANT TO COME TO THIS ETERNAL FLAME OF DIVINE FELLOWSHIP AND MINGLED LOVE?

There is a nearness that involves pain, rejection and persecution for righteousness sake. Christ states, "Blessed are those who have been persecuted for the sake of righteousness, for theirs is the Kingdom of Heaven. Blessed are you when people insult you and persecute you, and falsely say all kinds of evil against you because of Me. Rejoice and be glad, for your reward in heaven is great..." Matt. 5:10-12.

If nearness to Christ is our goal, then suffering for His name's sake will be part of the journey. As pilgrims here on the earth we will cut against the grain of what is normal and acceptable; even in the religious circles we may travel in. The question then is whether or not we are willing to drink the cup and participate in His sufferings.

In the first two years of being a believer I found myself excommunicated from two churches. This caused a depth of pain I can barely describe. My greatest joy was God and His people and yet I found myself rejected and discarded by those that I loved. All my friends, all my mentors, everyone whom I had loved and cherished rejected me, totally and completely. Again, I cannot describe the depth of pain I experienced in that place.

I remember when the Lord told us to move to Lynchburg to plant a House of Prayer and a church community. I remember running out of money and running out of food. I remember making our last box of macaroni and cheese for my children with a can of coconut milk I found in my cupboard. I don't ever remember buying that can of milk, but I praise God that I had it. I made the box of macaroni and cheese and added a small amount of leftover ground beef. I stirred it together and gave it to my children. I thought, "Well, that's it. We are going to eat this and die." At that very same time there was a prayer meeting going on at our church community and people on crutches were getting healed and the Presence of God was falling with all sorts of miracles taking place. I remember thinking, "God, it seems like you like what is going on down here. You are healing the sick and performing miracles. Can you provide food for my family?"

Moments like these, and so much more, are the moments where we say, "Yes" to drinking the cup that Jesus drank. Some commentators will tell you the cup represents martyrdom. But Jesus spoke these words to James and John. John is the only apostle known who was not martyred, and yet Jesus told them, "My cup you shall drink."

This cup is a cup of intimacy, but it is not for the faint of heart. This cup allows us to enter into greater communion with Christ as we share in His sufferings. It is the suffering that is born out of doing the right thing. It is pain born out of conformity to His image and his likeness. It is clear that there is no reward for suffering for our own sinful actions (1 Pet. 4:15), yet there is great reward in suffering hardship for the sake of His name and His glory, for, "If you are reviled for the name of Christ, you are blessed, because the Spirit of glory and of God rests on you." 1 Pet. 4:14.

Paul writes on how this godly suffering, godly hardship, this cup mixed with intimacy and pain is a door into a greater knowledge of who Christ is. He writes, "that I may know Him and the power of His resurrection and the fellowship of His sufferings, being conformed to His death; in order that I may attain to the resurrection from the dead." Phil. 3:10-11.

About a year ago our church was in the middle of a genuine outpouring of the Holy Spirit. His Presence and His Glory descended upon our congregation unlike anything that we have ever experienced. For eight weeks we met five times a week. We would gather and begin our meetings with 45 minutes to an hour of testimonies. So many testimonies! People were being saved, healed and delivered. I would often interrupt the testimonies and simply say, "Who here came here tonight to get right with God?" People would raise their hands and then stand up to receive Christ as their Lord and Savior.

One night, in the middle of this outpouring the Lord was doing an incredible thing. A fiery love filled the room. The church rushed to the front of the altar and laid face down. People were weeping, travailing and crying out to the Lord. For over an hour it seemed as the Lord was baptizing us with fire. A wave of fire and power would crash over us like a wave only to recede to then have another wave crash over us. We wept and cried and said yes to Jesus on a deeper level than before.

In the midst of this atmosphere the Lord spoke to me, "Jeff, I am going to Golgotha. Will you go with me?" I was stunned. I had never heard the Lord say anything of this kind to me before. Would I go to Golgotha? Would I go to the place where they crucified my Lord? What could I say? I said the only thing I could think of, "Yes Lord. Yes! I will go with you!"

As my yes came forth, out of my spirit instantly the Lord began to speak. To the degree that I was willing to lay down my life in love was the degree that He would raise me up with power. That I would have fellowship with Christ in His death, that I might share in His resurrection and power.

The loneliness that Christ experienced on His way to the cross but also His journey here on earth could relate and bridge the gap and correspond to any bit of loneliness I might ever feel in saying yes again on this journey of knowing Christ and being conformed to His image.

Power is for those who have died. Those who have said yes to knowing Christ even in the fire of rejection and misunderstanding. Family may fail and friends may fail but praise be to God, Jesus Christ our savior never fails.

This blessed cup of intimacy and rejection. This blessed cup of communion and pain. This blessed cup of the knowledge of God and the acquaintance of suffering is a cup that you and I are still beckoned to drink.

"We want to be with you where you are Jesus! We want to sit to your left and to your right!"

"Are you able to drink the cup that I must drink?" He replies.

"Yes, we are able!"

"You are right. My cup you will indeed drink."

May it be so. May our hearts say "Yes" to every drop of invitation to Presence and transformation. May our willingness to lay low equal the magnitude of intimacy, friendship and power.

All of us, for all of you. We will drink the cup.

LETTER THREE

AN ANGEL OF REVIVAL

"And He was saying to them, 'The harvest is plentiful, but the laborers are few; therefore beseech the Lord of the harvest to send out laborers into His harvest." Luke. 10:2.

"The harvest is the end of the age, and the harvesters are angels" Matt. 13:39.

IT HAD BEEN A VERY HARD YEAR.

Five years into planting our church community had passed. In that time, we had grown from 6 people in a living room to a couple hundred people. We had planted a church in a neighboring city as well as one in South Africa. We had been able to miraculously purchase our own building and were expecting nothing but good things. The Lord even provided food for my family – we didn't die. Thank you, Jesus,!

In spring of 2015 things began to unravel and the enemy began to sow dissension in the community. Different individuals began to leave and with them they spread accusations against my wife and I. A few dozen people left at one time and the church we had planted in the city next to us informed us that they no longer wanted to be associated with us.

We were hurting.

During this time, I was asked by my pastor and spiritual father to go to South Africa with him to minister at a pastor's conference. It was an opportunity I couldn't pass up and so I packed my things and flew to

Johannesburg, South Africa.

God moved powerfully while we were there, and it was refreshing to simply hear my pastor Charles Stock preach and minister. I was being touched and encouraged. I too was able to preach and minister and shared some of the story of what we had just walked through. My pain became bread for others to eat and many of the pastors were touched and refreshed by the Presence of God while we were there.

During this trip I had the opportunity for a private time of prayer. I sat in my room with my bible in front of me and began to read and pray. There was not an especially powerful sense of God's Presence, but I leaned into His heart on purpose and with the intention to interact with His Word and His Spirit afresh that day.

As I read and prayed, I began to sense that something shifted in the room. I suddenly became aware that an angel was standing at the foot of my bed. I did not see it with my natural eyes. The heavens weren't "opened" in front of me nor would I describe it as an overtly profound or demonstrative encounter. I perceived and discerned that an angel was present.

"For though by this time you ought to be teachers, you need someone to teach you again the first principles of the oracles of God; and you have come to need milk and not solid food. For everyone who partakes only of milk is unskilled in the word of righteousness, for he is a babe. But solid food belongs to those who are of full age, that is, those who by reason of use have their senses exercised to discern both good and evil." (Heb. 5:12-14).

I asked the Lord, "God, what is this angel?" I heard Him reply, "This is an angel of revival and you are taking him back to America." This may sound irreverent or trite but I simply replied, "Ok". I didn't know what to say really. I limped and dragged myself to South Africa having gotten beat up and betrayed by individuals whom I loved and cared for. I was accused of having motives different than what was actually true and I watched individuals and families break fellowship and participate in gossip and slander and hurt the community of God that we were pastoring. The last thing I was thinking about at that moment was an angel of revival or outpouring or anything of the like! I was thinking more about surviving the storm.

Upon returning to America I didn't tell many people about my encounter. I told my wife, and my associate at church and a good friend. I didn't tell the congregation and I didn't put it on social media. My thought was that if the encounter was real and legitimate then I wouldn't have to tell everyone that I was given an angel of revival from South Africa back to the States!

"Like clouds and wind without rain is the one who boasts falsely about his gifts" (Prov. 25:14).

I remember the first time reading that verse where the Lord spoke to me through it and I said, "Lord, I don't want to be that guy! I don't want to have a reputation I can't fulfill! I would rather be the guy who is understated but can bring the wind and the rain and the thunder and the lightening!" That may be an immature attitude but I will let the Lord be the judge of that. It has been a personal conviction and something that I have tried to live out. In the same vein I know the Word says, "Let another praise you, and not your own mouth; a stranger, and not your own lips" (Prov. 27:2).

That was January 2016. I returned home encouraged by the ministry that I was both able to participate in and receive. Having shared that encounter with about 3 people, I went back to pastoring the church. Two months had passed by and honestly, I had pretty much forgotten about that angelic encounter. We were preparing for an event at our church called Awaken Love. It is a weeklong immersive internship and conference for young adults, and it is always a powerful time.

That year's speakers included Matt Gilman who had been an integral part of the House of Prayer in Kansas City and as of this writing is a leader in the Orlando House of Prayer. What was significant about that was that about 7 years prior, my wife JoAnna had a dream that involved Matt Gilman. In the dream she saw a worship service occurring in a large rectangular building and during the service revival was breaking out. This dream occurred before we moved to Lynchburg, before we started our church, and before our church ended up purchasing a former roller-skating rink which is in the shape of a large rectangle! The week before the event began, I went to sleep and found myself in an encounter.

I was in the spirit and outside of my body in my bedroom. I was floating above the headboard of my bed and could see my wife and myself asleep in our room. As I lifted my attention to look around the room, I saw two angels standing at the foot of my bed. These two angels were both holding long silver trumpets. In unison they lifted their trumpets and gave a simultaneous blast. As the sound went forth, I was thrusted into my body and woke up. However, I did not wake up out of the encounter. I merely woke up in the dream and now was in my body and awake and staring at the end of a trumpet that was blasting in my face.

I was completely overwhelmed as the noise and the presence of these heavenly beings filled the room. In awe and overwhelm I simply sat there trembling under the Presence of God. When the trumpet blasts were finished, the two angels returned to the Lord and I was left there alone and confused. I did not understand the encounter and I did not understand what was to happen next. As I sat there in my bed still overcome by the angelic visitors and the trumpet blasts, I turned my head to my right and noticed that another angel was now present in my room.

Standing to the right of my bed he began to speak to me about Heaven and things that were about to take place. He would speak to me, and then leave, only to return and then speak to me again. This went on for what would feel like all night long. The things that the angel spoke to me about stunned me and when I awoke, I could not find the words to describe what he had spoken to me save one thing.

He told me that at this present time there was a group of angels who were being trained in Heaven to minister to those who were victims of childhood sexual abuse. He informed me that these angels were about to be released to the earth and that help was coming.

This was the only thing that he said to me that I could articulate when I awoke and yet I remember being somewhat offended in the encounter when he told me this. Why aren't the angels here now? Why are we waiting? Why hasn't God done something already? These were the questions that were swirling in my spirit during that encounter. I would later resolve all of these questions with the simple acknowledgement that God's ways are not our ways (Is. 55:8). Why would an omnipresent God need angels anyway? Why would an omnipotent God need angels? Why would a God who describes Himself as The Word need someone to speak for Him? These are all somewhat in the realm of mystery and yet this is the reality that is revealed to us in the Word of God. Our job is not to evaluate God's ways but to humbly submit to them and acknowledge them as good.

I woke up that morning speaking in tongues and filled with the Holy Ghost.

A few days later during a worship service with Matt Gilman leading worship in our large rectangular building, **revival broke out**. An outrageous and heavy Presence of God filled the room and remained for the next eight weeks. This visitation erupted and we began meeting together at the church five times a week. Every meeting was filled with powerful salvations, healings and deliverance. God spoke with such clarity and such power that no one could deny His activity.

As I pondered my visitation with the angels, I began to recollect Zechariah 4. "Now the angel who talked with me came back and wakened me, as a man who is wakened out of his sleep." Zech. 4:1. In the encounter I was asleep in bed and the angels awoke me out of my sleep. These were angels of awakening.

About a week later I remembered that there was something about silver trumpets in the Bible. I just couldn't remember where. After a little bit of searching I found they are described in Numbers 10. "The Lord spoke further to Moses, saying, 'Make yourself two trumpets of silver, of hammered work you shall make them; and you shall use them for summoning the congregation and for having the camps set out. When both are blown, all the congregation shall gather themselves to you at the doorway of the tent of meeting. Yet if only one is blown, then the leaders, the heads of the divisions of Israel, shall assemble before you'" (Num. 10:1-4).

It was clear: The angels were angels of awakening that were blowing the silver trumpets which releases an anointing to gather the people of God. For eight weeks people from all over our city would come into the meetings. Unbelievers, Christians, pastors and leaders would all attend. Even people from the surrounding region drove several hours to come and get touched by God.

The encounter in South Africa with an angel of revival was real. God had visited me and revival was indeed breaking out.

"After these things I looked, and behold, a door standing open in heaven, and the first voice which I had heard, like the sound of a trumpet speaking with me, said, 'Come up here, and I will show you what must take place after these things,'" Rev. 4:1.

This testimony of prophetic and angelic encounters holds the power to release more of the same in those who hear of it, "For the testimony of Jesus is the spirit of prophecy." Rev. 19:10. Even as you have read this story, a seed of faith has been deposited in your heart to receive the same. May God's activity in your life be activated and increased like never before and may the mighty hand of God and His holy angels work with you that Jesus Christ may be glorified!

LETTER FOUR

DRAWING NEAR TO GOD

"Draw near to God, and He will draw near to you" James 4:8.

Prior to moving to Virginia, when I lived in Pennsylvania, I was working full time as a manager at a car dealership that was an hour away from my house. Most days are twelve-hour workdays. You get there at 8:30am and you leave at 9:00pm or later. Add an hour drive each way and you can begin to understand the intensity of that schedule.

My wife would pack me a lunch before I left and would pray for me as she did it.

It was a perplexing season for she and I. About a year and a half earlier we were in Annapolis MD where both sides of our family lived. We had purchased a home and started a family. I was in the car industry then too and had done very well for a young 20 something.

Having been unsuccessful to find a church community that was pursing God and revival, our solution was to drive to a church that was. The church that we found happened to be two hours away. So, for three years we would wake up very early on Sunday morning to be on the road by 8:30am. That would ensure that we would arrive by 10:30am and could make our way to the front of the church to be ready to worship when the service began at 10:45am. God would show up, we would get wrecked by the love of God and stirred up to believe God for more than we could ask, think or imagine. The atmosphere was electric, and it was in that atmosphere that God define what a "normal church" really looked like.

In the middle of all of that the Lord spoke to me in a dream: I wasn't pursuing the call of God on my life. He had called us to travel and be revivalists. He had called us to be consecrated to His purposes in this generation and to see a harvest around the world. We heard His call and responded. We sold our home, quit my job, got rid of a bunch of our stuff and moved to Harrisburg PA without the slightest idea of what would come next.

For the next year I would spend my time picking up golf balls from 5am-12pm and then ride my bike back home to my wife and kids. I would then drive downtown to work in an inner-city ministry and then come home for dinner. On nights and weekends, we would travel and speak and worship and preach anywhere that there was an invitation to do so. During that time, we met a brand-new church plant that asked us to move to D.C. to help their new congregation. We decided it was the Lord and so we moved once again.

However, in order to live in that area, I would need to get a good paying job. Church plants don't have a lot of extra income for salaries and I would have to earn a living a different way. Almost a year and a half after leaving everything, I would go back to the car business. Having given up our home and our family and our stuff, I would have to return to what I wanted to leave, just without all the fun stuff to go along with it!

Day after day I drove to work. Most of the time perplexed and puzzled as to why after asking us to leave everything that He had called us back into what He had told us to leave. Time was not a commodity that was available in that season and my heart longed for more of God's Presence and friendship. I was hungry and thirsty for God. I remember driving to work praying, "God! I am hungry and thirsty for you! I long to be touched by you and filled by you. I am hungry for more of you". During that day I had my own little revelation: "I can't devote hours and hours to pray to you every day with the schedule that I am working. But, I can fast."

Immediately a supernatural grace for fasting fell upon my life. I began fasting as a lifestyle. I would eat a meal and skip the next three, then eat again and skip a few more. I would eat, fast for the next two days and then eat again. It became as natural and easy as riding a bike and when this supernatural grace for fasting fell on my life I didn't have to think about it or convince myself to keep going. Something inside of me was compelling me to fast and seek the face of God.

The nearness of God became more and more real. My life schedule hadn't changed. My responsibilities and duties hadn't changed. But something inside of me had changed and I was being propelled into a season of intense nearness to God through fasting. I was drawing near to God and He was drawing near to me.

I found my solace in doing the "little things" for God during this season. My assignment was to manage a car dealership and so I did my work "as unto the Lord." (Col. 3:23). Menial tasks became worship as my heart was more fully alive and present to God's reality. It didn't matter if it was answering emails, innovating and working on items that would improve processes around the dealership, or simply locking gates and shutting down the store after it was closed. Every action was set upon an altar and God was the object of my affection.

It was during this time that the Lord supernaturally moved me out of the car industry once again. My wife JoAnna and I found ourselves in Kansas City seeking the Lord for direction and leading. I had been living this lifestyle of extreme fasting for several months and secretly had felt like the Lord was about to call me into an extended fast, something I had never done before. As we sought the Lord in prayer, He spoke to me out of the book of Daniel: I was to do a 21 day fast. Almost immediately I began this extended fast. The Presence of God was sweet to my heart and we were thrilled because God was speaking, and things were moving in the heavens and on earth.

During this time the Lord spoke that we were to start a house of prayer. This seed, this dream was the beginning of what would ultimately lead to us relocating from Maryland to Lynchburg, Virginia in order to pursue this dream. God used this "drawing near" to "draw near to me" in the form of fasting. My heart reached new levels of sensitivity and passion for the Presence of God in the midst of very demanding circumstances.

Drawing near to God. "You will seek Me and find Me when you search for Me with all your heart" (Jer. 29:13). "Draw near to God, and He will draw near to you" (Jas. 4:8). "Let us draw near with a sincere heart in full assurance of faith..." (Heb. 10:22). Scriptures such as these and so many others speak to the hunger within to draw near. We have been brought near by the blood, but now that we have been brought near, do we ourselves draw near? Are we satisfied with our level of encounter and friendship with God, or do we long to draw nearer still? The Word of God speaks to you and I.

Draw near to Him, and He will draw near to you.

LETTER FIVE

LOVING GOD MORE DEEPLY

Coming to Christ as I did, I often think that I had an advantage in my walk with Him. I was so broken, so thirsty, so desperate for change and freedom in my life, every drop of God's Presence and God's Word was treasured like the costliest of gems. I had come out of a life of brokenness and torment and found that the only peace I found was when I would keep an internal dialogue going with God.

Now, I am not saying that I would speak to the Lord and then I would hear an audible or internal voice speaking back to me. Rather I would speak to God and as I did, I would feel a tangible Presence of love, peace and security. I would come to know this Presence as the Holy Spirit Himself and would cherish this gift of God above all others. I learned what it meant to "pray without ceasing" (1 Thess. 5:17). It was not a discipline driven by religious zeal, it was my life, my breath, my everything. As I was trained in experiencing God's Presence, I would seek out times to give myself more wholly and completely to Him.

I found that I could experience God in incredible ways walking through the halls of my High School or serving tables at the local restaurant where I worked after school. I remember one day where I was in the kitchen at this restaurant and keeping this internal dialogue going with the Lord. As I did His Presence began to increase and increase and increase. It took everything within me not to fall to my knees and weep as His Presence visited me powerfully in that kitchen. Because He met me so powerfully in the everyday busyness of life, it was natural that I would seek more dedicated times that did not include distractions in order to interact with God.

As I mentioned before, I would go home and head to my room. Sitting on my floor with my Bible opened before me I would stretch out my hands like I was going to receive a gift and pray, "God I'm here. I want to know you. Would you come and meet with me?" As I did this, a waterfall of liquid love would begin to flow and crash over me. I would feel His love and affection and peace crashing over my heart. I remember the first time I read David's words, "Deep calls to deep at the sound of Your waterfalls; All Your breakers and Your waves have rolled over me." Psalm 42:7.

My heart leapt inside my chest, "Yes! That's it! I'm experiencing what David was experiencing!" A deep sense of solidarity began to rise within my heart that I served the same God as Abraham, Isaac, and Jacob. I was experiencing the same Presence that Moses, and Joshua and David was experiencing. I was interacting with the same Word that Isaiah and Jeremiah and Ezekiel interacted with. I was being filled with the same power that Peter, James, John and the rest of the apostles were filled with. My heart cry began to be formed into the same heart cry of Paul, "I count all things to be loss in view of the surpassing value of knowing Christ Jesus my Lord, for whom I have suffered the loss of all things, and count them but rubbish so that I may gain Christ." Phil. 3:8.

All of this was born out of experience; personal, intimate interaction with the Creator of the Universe. Many believers can quote John 3:16, "For God so loved the world, that he gave His only begotten son, that whoever believes in Him shall not perish, but have eternal life." This speaks of eternal life and how to obtain it and is indispensable and undeniably paramount to our faith. But how many believers know John 17:3 where Christ explains what eternal life is? "This is eternal life, that they may know You, the only true God, and Jesus Christ whom You have sent." John 17:3.

This "Knowing God" is the language of lovers and not intellectually driven. It is for those whom every lover of God throughout every generation have been able to identify with. It is for the hungry, the desperate, the poor in spirit, the forsaken and the outcast. It is for those who have no other good within themselves besides the good that the Father has deposited. They are dependent, despondent with any other answer or reality. It is the life that begins here on earth and continues into eternity.

Eternal life is not something that happens when our mortal body passes away. It is an intimate love relationship with the Father, Son, and Holy Spirit that begins the moment we are born again and continues into eternity. It begins here on earth and continues into heaven. It is the highest and loftiest calling any human being can obtain. Kings, princes, CEO's and billionaires are poor and bankrupt without this reality, and the beggars and children of slums are rich when it is present.

It is the key and the door to every spiritual blessing. It is more powerful than our past experiences and more powerful than what we think we know is true. Relationship with God is the invitation of the ages. It is the opportunity of a lifetime and it is passed over by the worldly and religious alike. Relationship with God is the fountain from which true spirituality and true Christianity springs, and it is still calling and drawing us today. My initial encounters with God began in the Spring of 2001. As I write this it is the spring of 2017. The same fire that warmed my heart then is beckoning me deeper still today.

There is a form of spirituality that would have us drink just a little from this fountain of eternal life and then have us turn away. We may have drunk enough to have the most basic of our thirst quenched, yet we neglect to continue to drink in order that we might be changed and transformed into the image of His Son.

God's Presence is so overwhelming, so amazing, we may begin to drink of it and walk with Him out of desperation, healing, and need much as I did as a young man. But God's desire is that this overwhelming Presence would begin to mold and shape and form Christ in us. That we would throw off "childish things" and begin to mature as sons and daughters of the Most High God. That we would begin to desire what He wants because it is what He wants and not merely because of how we feel. In this way, we continue to wade into the river that flows from the throne (Rev. 22:1) to the point where we are overtaken by His desires and no longer able to merely forge ahead in our own strengths and pursuits (Ez. 45:7).

Eternal Life. Relationship with God.

This has been the cry of the ancients and the fathers and mothers who have gone before us. It is the heart cry of prophets and holy men and women of old. It is the cry of reformers and revivalists. It is the cry of the poor and spiritually broken and it is the cry of the heart of God for you and me.

Will you answer the cry?

You have said "Yes" to God once. Will you say "Yes" to Him again today? And tomorrow? And after that?

Having drunk from the river of eternal life, we remain children, adolescents, never graduating and never moving on. We remain moldable, teachable and hungry to know Him more.

Won't you say yes to Him again today?

LETTER SIX

REWARDED BY GOD

"Slaves, be obedient to those who are your masters according to the flesh, with fear and trembling, in sincerity of your heart, as to Christ; not by way of eyeservice, as men-pleasers, but as slaves of Christ, doing the will of God from the heart. With good will render service, as to the Lord, and not to men, knowing that whatever good thing each one does, this he will receive back form the Lord, whether slave or free." Ephesians 6:5-8

My wife and I had moved with our two kids to outside the D.C. beltway to help with a church plant. For the first year, I went back to the car business to fund our mission. I was working as a Manager and I worked long hours and tried to do my best. Things shifted and I wanted more flexibility for ministry. For me, that looked like going back to the only other industry I really knew - restaurants.

A burger place within walking distance from my house was hiring servers so I applied and was hired. I got a schedule that ended up being around 36 hours a week. Sometimes it was a little more and rarely was it less, but it was vastly less than the hours I was putting in at the car dealership. This allowed me to put more of myself into where my real passion was - ministry.

I was an associate pastor at the church plant we were working with, leading worship, prayer meetings, serving as a youth pastor and fully invested in the "extra" work that accompanies a church start-up.

One of the things that usually accompanies a church start-up is a lack of funds and so that is where serving tables fit in. My wife and I moved our family into a basement apartment with no kitchen. Things were pretty intense. My wife would wash our dishes in the bathroom sink and most of our meals revolved around a microwave if we wanted our meal warm. We were sacrificing for the gospel. My wife JoAnna would often say things like, "If we were living as missionaries in some third world country, I would have to do things harder than this, so who am I to complain?" While we were pressing into the Lord, we felt that our sacrifices would not go unseen.

During this time, I realized that while serving was bringing in some income, perhaps there was another role within the restaurant that paid more that might be available to me. I had worked in restaurants since I was 15 and I had managed people at car dealerships, so in my mind I was the perfect candidate for a promotion at the burger place. I asked my boss if I could speak to him for a moment and what came next was a conversation that I will remember for the rest of my life.

My boss was an immigrant from a south American country. He was two years younger than me and about a foot shorter than I am. Or at least we started the conversation with me being taller, but I am sure it ended with me being about an inch off the ground.

I told my boss that while being in restaurant management wasn't really "my goal in life" I felt like I was "open" to a promotion within the restaurant. I told him that if there was a position that paid more, I would like to discuss what that option may look like to see how I could get compensated higher than what I made serving tables.

It was 2009 and America was in the depths of what is now known as the Great Recession. Work was really hard to come by and jobs were at a premium in any industry. What I didn't realize was that the Lord was about to rebuke me through the mouth of my unbelieving supervisor.

With his eyes suddenly turning a shade of red and his demeanor flipping into "hostile territory" he replied to me: "You want a raise?! You want a promotion?! You would be the last person in the restaurant that I would consider! There are people here who work harder than you, better than you and are more thankful for the job that they have! I would never give you a promotion!" And the beating went on and on. I literally felt myself shrinking to the floor as the truth of my sin was revealed.

The truth is, I did despise serving "smiling burgers and famous shakes." I felt like the job was beneath me and I had justified a bad attitude towards my employment because serving burgers "wasn't my calling."

"Whether, then you eat or drink or whatever you do, do all to the glory of God." 1 Corinthians 10:31.

"So, Joseph found favor in [Potiphar's] sight and became his personal servant; and he made him overseer over his house, and all that he owned he put on his charge. It came about that from the time he made him overseer in his house and over all that he owned, the Lord blessed the Egyptian's house on account of Joseph: thus the Lord's blessing was upon all that he owned, in the house and in the field. So he left everything he owned in Joseph's charge; and with him there he did not concern himself with anything except the food which he ate." Genesis 39:4-6.

"And if you have not been faithful in the use of that which is another's, who will give you that which is your own?" Luke 16:2.

"**With good will render service, as to the Lord**, and not to men, knowing that **whatever good thing each one does, this he will receive back form the Lord**, whether slave or free." Ephesians 6:7-8 Emphasis Mine

When I left for my walk home that day, I did some business with the Lord. I prayed: "Lord, I've sinned. I've despised my work, and I have dishonored my boss. I have not given him my best. It's sin and I repent. Today it changes. I am going to treat my work like I am working for you. I am going to pour myself into it. If something is important to my boss, then I am going to make it important to me. Today everything changes."

The next time I walked into that restaurant, I treated it like I was in the ministry position of my dreams. I poured myself into my work and I communicated through my actions that I honored the job and honored the role.

For me, that looked like the little things that I used to scoff at in my heart. In the restaurant I worked for, they had rules about how many sugars, Equals, and Sweet 'N Lows went into a sugar caddy. It was something like 6 sugars, 5 Equals, and 4 Sweet 'N Lows. These were the things that I would skim over because I would say to myself, "What is the difference? Who cares as long as the caddy is full?!"

You know who cared? My boss. You know who else cared? Jesus Christ. Ephesians tells us to work as unto the Lord and not as if it was just a man you were serving.

Suddenly every time I swept the floor, it became worship to the Lord. Every time I followed some "weird or unnecessary" rule that the restaurant had, I was doing it unto Christ. My fellowship deepened. My intimacy expanded. I was entrusting myself to the Lord in my service to an unbelieving boss, making what was important to my boss important to me regardless of whether I understood the significance or reasoning behind the rules. I began communicating honor and respect through my actions knowing that, "whatever good thing each one does, this he will receive back form the Lord".

I got a revelation that nothing gets lost...ever. No matter whether you are serving a pagan, demon worshipping slave owner like Potiphar in Egypt, or an "old fashioned" pastor in your local church. If you posture your heart to honor and respect those that are over you, Jesus Christ Himself receives it as worship. He receives it as worship and He Himself will make sure you are rewarded. That reward may come through the place that you are serving or it may come further down the road but, "do not be deceived, God is not mocked; for whatever a man sows, this he will also reap" Galatians 6:7.

Within months I got a promotion and a raise. Within a year I was ready to move to Lynchburg to plant the church community I currently serve. On my last day of working and serving "smiling burgers and famous shakes," I was the last server in the restaurant that night. I remember where I was in the restaurant sweeping the floor as my manager came to me. "Don't go," he began, "we are opening up another location in just a few months. I will make you the assistant General Manager and then you will be positioned for another promotion shortly after that."

I had to graciously decline what I had so forcefully tried to obtain just a year earlier. I had been serving Christ everywhere except in regard to my employment. When I repented of my sin and turned my heart towards the Lord and towards my supervisors, favor and grace began pouring back onto my life. It opened the door to favor and increase within my workplace and favor and grace in regard to the dreams of my heart.

God used my unbelieving boss to rebuke me and speak prophetically into my life. It changed me forever and I will never be the same.

LETTER SEVEN

THE FEAR OF THE LORD

"The fear of the Lord is the beginning of wisdom. And the knowledge of the Holy One is understanding." *Proverbs 9:10*

"The fear of the Lord is clean, enduring forever; the judgements of the Lord are true; they are righteous altogether." *Psalm 19:9*

"The secret of the Lord is for those who fear Him, and he will make them know His covenant." *Psalm 25:14*

TO KNOW THE FEAR OF THE LORD.

The fear of the Lord. The knowledge of God. To behold Him in His beauty and to see Him in the splendor of His might. To know Him. Not simply the parts of Him that seem desirable or comfortable, but all of Him. Every part. To know and be known by Him; no filters and no substitutes.

It had been an amazing season for JoAnna and I. We had, based on a series of prophetic words and dreams, quit my job, sold our home and many of our possessions to move to Harrisburg PA to pursue our calling in ministry. We moved into a small 2-bedroom townhome and we would seek the Lord daily. After several months, the Lord led me to get a job picking up golf balls at a local driving range. I also got a job working at an inner-city ministry leading an after-school classroom for at risk kids.

"You'll be picking up golf balls from 6am-1pm" my new boss told me. That was going to be a problem for me because I was supposed to be at my job with the inner-city ministry at 1pm. "Can I work from 5am-Noon?" I asked. "I don't care what time you get here just as long as the balls are picked up by 1pm," he gruffly replied. Fair enough. 5am it would be.

For me that looked like getting up at 4am to get dressed and ready to leave my house by 4:30. We had sold our nice cars and bought an old corolla. If I drove it to the driving range, then JoAnna would be stuck at home all day with our young son and no way to go to the grocery store or anywhere else. I bought a bike from Walmart for $50 and it became my primary transportation.

Before moving to Harrisburg, PA, I had been managing two dealerships, drove a brand-new company car with custom wheels and everything paid for. Now I rode a bike to work... to pick up golf balls... at 4:30 in the morning.

I would drive my bike through the brisk night air. I found a small flashlight that I wrapped around the handlebars of my bike. I let it hang off the handlebars swinging to and fro as I drove. It made a type of helicopter pattern on the ground and I hoped that it would be enough for an earlier morning traveler to see and avoid clipping me on the side of the road. After a few close calls I deciding to be more proactive so when I saw or heard a car coming, I would pick up the flashlight with one hand and frantically click it on and off in the direction of the car.

Thug-ministry-life, I guess.

Everything I did was focused towards stepping into this season of seeking the Lord with abandonment. We desired to be used by God and we were trying to tell the Lord this in everything that was set before us. I would spend hours seeking the Lord whenever I could. I continued to ask the Lord to burn eternity on my eyes. About a year earlier I had gotten sucked out of my body and taken to the heavenly Jerusalem. I saw the Lord Jesus Christ as the Jewish man, fully God and fully man. He had brown hair, brown eyes, a brown beard and dark skin. That encounter forever changed me and marked me concerning the reality of the unseen world and the power of the supernatural activity of Heaven. Jesus Christ was about to visit me again, but it was to be in a much different way.

"And behold, two of them were going that very day to a village named Emmaus, which was about seven miles from Jerusalem. And they were talking with each other about all these things which had taken place. While they were talking and discussing, Jesus Himself approached and began traveling with them. But their eyes were prevented from recognizing Him." Luke 24:13-16

"But Mary was standing outside the tomb weeping; and so, as she wept, she stooped and looked into the tomb; and she saw two angels in white sitting, one at the head and one at the feet, where the body of Jesus had been lying. And they said to her, 'Woman, why are you weeping?' She said to them, 'Because they have taken away my Lord, and I do not know where they have laid Him.' When she had said this, she turned around and saw Jesus standing there, and did not know that it was Jesus. Jesus said to her, 'Woman, why are you weeping? Whom are you seeking?' Supposing Him to be the gardener, she said to Him, 'Sir, if you have carried Him away, tell me where you have laid Him, and I will take Him away.' Jesus said to her, 'Mary!' She turned and said to Him in Hebrew, 'Rabboni!' (which means, Teacher). John 20:11-16

"Then I turned to see the voice that was speaking with me. And having turned I saw seven golden lampstands; and in the middle of the lampstands I saw one like a son of man, clothed in a robe reaching to the feet, and girded across His chest with a golden sash. His head and His hair were white like white wool, like snow; and His eyes were like a flame of fire. His feet were like burnished bronze, when it has been made to glow in a furnace, and His voice was like the sound of many waters. In His right hand he held seven stars, and out of His mouth came a sharp two-edged sword; and His face was like the sun shining in its strength." Revelation 1:12-16

"Then I began to weep greatly because no one was found worthy to open the book or to look into it; and one of the elders said to me, 'Stop weeping; behold, the Lion that is from the tribe of Judah, the Root of David, has overcome so as to open the book and its seven seals.' And I saw between the throne (with the four living creatures) and the elders a Lamb standing, as if slain, having seven horns and seven eyes, which are the seven Spirits of God, set out into all the earth. And He came and took the book out of the right hand of Him who sat on the throne." Revelation 5:4-7

Before taking me to Heaven, the Lord had tried to draw me into encounters several times. Each time, as I felt my spirit leave my body and begin to fly through space, I panicked and allowed fear to grip me. I resisted and told the Lord to stop. Each time, He honored my request, putting me safely back into my body and wholly without the encounter that He desired for me.

My fear and unbelief raged against the purposes of God. I could feel this natural tendency toward these things and began purposing in my heart that I would stay in faith and stay in trust. "Even if it kills me God," I prayed, "I will not reject you when you come to me." I began building up my spirit through prayer and the Word to recognize Christ when He came to me and to reject fear and unbelief.

Once again, I found myself asleep and in an encounter.

"But when he had considered this, behold, **an angel of the Lord appeared to him in a dream,** saying, 'Joseph, son of David, do not be afraid to take Mary as your wife; for the Child who has been conceived in her is of the Holy Spirit." Matthew 1:20

"Indeed God speaks once, or twice, yet no one notices it. In a dream, a vision of the night, when sound sleep falls on men, while they slumber in their beds, then He opens the ears of men, and seals their instruction, that He may turn man aside from his conduct, and keep man from pride; He keeps back his soul from the pit, and his life from passing over into Sheol." Job 33:14-18

"Jacob left Beersheba and set out for Harran. When he reached a certain place, he stopped for the night because the sun had set. Taking one of the stones there, he put it under his head and lay down to sleep. **He had a dream** in which he saw a stairway resting on the earth, with its top reaching to heaven, and the angels of God were ascending and descending on it. There above it stood the Lord, and he said: "I am the Lord, the God of your father Abraham and the God of Isaac. I will give you and your descendants the land on which you are lying. Your descendants will be like the dust of the earth, and you will spread out to the west and to the east, to the north and to the south. All peoples on earth will be blessed through you and your offspring. I am with you and will watch over you wherever you go, and I will bring you back to this land. I will not leave you until I have done what I have promised you.' When Jacob awoke from his sleep, he thought, 'Surely the Lord is in this place, and I was not aware of it.' He was afraid and said, 'How awesome is this place! This is none other than the house of God; this is the gate of heaven."

Genesis 28:10-17

I found myself standing in a field.

It was dark around me but off in the distance I could see a large building pulsating with energy. As I peered closely, I could see that the structure was being encircled by angels like a molecule is encircled with electrons. While the sight was incredible to me, there was nothing else really happening. The building was a far way off and I was simply standing in a field. Then suddenly it appeared.

A glowing red hue appeared about 15 feet away from me. It was faint and only a foot or so off of the ground. Before I could even think about it I found myself blurting out, "That's you and I know it!"

Suddenly the glowing red light began moving. Slowly at first and then picking up speed it made a circle once, twice, and then over and over again. It began moving so quickly I couldn't make out the initial ball of light that I saw. The circular movement of the light now moved up so that it began to form a "pillar" of red light. Then suddenly… He was there.

Out of the pillar of red light emerged Jesus Christ the Victor and conquering King. He wore a robe of pure red. The color was so deep and vivid it is hard to even describe how red it really was. He was a Man on fire. His eyes burning with passion and His hair seemed to fly wildly around Him as if He was in a windstorm.

Looking into His face instilled instant fear. I fell on the ground and began to tremble.

"I was astonished," He said, "I was astonished as I look and found no man to help. So I tread the winepress alone."

He took a step towards me.

"There was no one to help so I tread the winepress alone!"

His voice was ripping through every molecule of my body. The only emotion I had in that moment was fear and dread.

"Jesus!" I cried out. "Jesus!"

He just kept walking and kept repeating. There was no one to help. He looked but found none. So he tread the winepress alone.

I kept screaming. He kept walking. "Jesus! Jesus! Jesus!"

What I didn't realize is that I was screaming in real life. I was in the encounter with the Lord, but in my bedroom asleep in the middle of the night, I was screaming the name of Jesus as loud as I could. My wife was obviously woken up by this process and naturally thought I was having a nightmare.

She tried to wake me with no success. "Jeff! Wake up!" But I was totally possessed by this image: Blood stained robe, eyes of fire, a man of war coming back from battle... The Lord Almighty is His name.

My wife sat up and began shaking me and screaming, "Jeff! Wake up!" And then I was back.

I was back, but I was changed.

I continued to tremble as my mind began to process what I had just encountered. Unable to fully explain it, after some time to just settle down, we went back to sleep.

The alarm clock seemed to go off early that night. As I rolled out of bed at 4 A.M. it took me but a moment to realize I was still in the encounter. Sure, I no longer was standing in the field and no longer saw the Lord, but it was as if my clothes still smelled like the smoke of the fire I was just in.

I could feel Him. I could feel the fear of the Lord like a cloud or an anointing. Maybe even more so like I had just had a signet permanently mark my soul.

I was still shaking when I woke up and as I made my way down the stairs to prepare for my day of picking up golf balls I was rapidly trying to process and understand what had just taking place.
I remember getting a bowl of cereal and sitting in my kitchen. For some reason I had remembered that a friend of mine had told me about a website that had a free audio version of the book of revelation. I grabbed my computer (still trying to finish my mini-wheats) and found the website. I randomly clicked on a section and thought that the scripture would settle me down.

I was wrong.

The voice began to emerge from my laptop saying this:

"And I saw heaven opened, and behold, a white horse, and He who sat on it is called Faithful and True, and in righteousness he judges and wages war. His eyes are a flame of fire, and on His head are many diadems; and

He has a name written on Him which no one knows except Himself. He is clothed with a robe dipped in blood, and His name is called The Word of God" (Revelation 19:11-13).

As soon as I heard, "He is clothed with a robe dipped in blood" my spoon literally fell out of my hand, I fell out of my chair, and hit the floor shaking once again saying, "Jesus! Jesus! Jesus!"

The voice continued:

"And the armies which are in heaven, clothed in fine linen, white and clean were following Him on white horses. From His mouth comes a sharp sword, so that with it He may strike down the nations, and He will rule them with a rod of iron; and He treads the wine press of the fierce wrath of God, the Almighty. And on his robe and on His thigh He has a name written, "KING OF KINGS, AND LORD OF LORDS" (Revelation 19:14-16).

I had seen Him. I saw the King. I saw the Lord Almighty the man of War who makes and wages war and who's robe is stained blood red.

I don't know how I got through work that day. Granted, picking up golf balls isn't the most intellectually taxing job but still, I felt like I was walking around in a stupor the whole day. Shaking some. Crying some. Worshipping some. I was more afraid of Jesus Christ than I had ever been in my entire life by like a factor of a thousand, but I also felt closer to Him and more in awe of Him and struck by the reality of who He IS, not simply who He WAS.

I would return home and I started flying through pages of the prophets. I knew this whole encounter was a reference to something in the Word, but I couldn't remember what or where. It was sometime later that week I found what I was looking for: Isaiah 63.

"Who is this who comes from Edom, with garments of glowing colors from Bozrah, this One who is majestic in His apparel, marching in the greatness of His strength? 'It is I who speak in righteousness, mighty to save.' Why is Your apparel red, and Your garments like the one who treads in the wine press? 'I have trodden the wine trough alone and from the peoples there was no man with Me. I also trod them in My anger and trampled them in My wrath; and their lifeblood is sprinkled on My garments, and I stained

all My raiment. For the day of vengeance was in My heart, and My year of redemption has come. I looked, and there was no one to help, and I was astonished and there was no one to uphold; so my own arm brought salvation to Me, and My wrath upheld Me. I trod down the peoples in My anger and made them drunk in My wrath, and I poured out their lifeblood on the earth. Isaiah 63:1-6.

I really had no words.

Slowly it began to sink in that somehow, I had entered into Isaiah's vision in a dream in the night. I hadn't been reading this passage or studying the book of Isaiah. I didn't even know what this passage said. But having experienced it for myself, I know instinctively it was somewhere in the Bible.

Jesus reveals Himself however He wants and in the manner that we need to perceive Him. I had perceived Him as a friend in His heavenly room several years early, but now I had received Him as the One who is majestic in His apparel and marching in the greatness of His strength. What I saw struck fear into the deepest part of who I am. I felt like I had been baptized into the fear of the Lord.

Eventually the shaking stopped. But the sense of His greatness and awesome splendor has not. He is the Lamb of God, but He is also the conquering King.

All hail King Jesus.

King of Kings, and Lord of Lords.

"For if we go on sinning willfully after receiving the knowledge of the truth, there no longer remains a sacrifice for sins, but a terrifying expectation of judgment and the fury of a fire which will consume the adversaries. Anyone who has set aside the Law of Moses dies without mercy on the testimony of two or three witnesses. How much severer punishment do you think he will deserve who has trampled under foot the Son of God, and has regarded as unclean the blood of the covenant by which he was sanctified and has insulted the Spirit of grace? For we know Him who said, 'Vengeance is Mine, I will repay.' And again, 'The Lord will judge His people.' It is a terrifying thing to fall into the hands of the living God." Hebrews 10:26-31

LETTER EIGHT

DO YOU LOVE ME?

REVIVAL

It had swept through our church like a hurricane or tornado that no one saw coming.

Following two angelic visitations, an eight-week revival exploded onto our church and thrusted us into 8 weeks of nightly meetings. Night after night His Presence was poured out onto our body and souls were beings saved, healed, and delivered.

It really did feel like heaven on earth and is honestly hard to even describe how incredible and overwhelming it all was. While it is going on there is this incredible mixture of wonder and awe mixed with celebration of what you are seeing in front of you, all seasoned with this fear of the Lord in that you don't want to "mess it up" or "lay hold of the ark."

Truly incredible.

However, after eight weeks of nightly meetings the services came to an end. As sudden and unexpected as its beginning was, so was its end.

Now, if you've been in a revival before you know this: you don't start revival. We can have gifts and anointings of all types. Some of these gifts and anointings are incredibly powerful and effective at bringing about salvations, healing and deliverance. But revival is not simply an increase of these things, it is a manifestation, appearing, or "tabernacling" of Jesus Christ Himself.

> *"And I saw the holy city, new Jerusalem, coming down out of heaven from God, made ready as a bride adorned for her husband. And I heard a loud voice from the throne, saying, 'Behold, the tabernacle of God is among men, and He will dwell among them, and they shall be His people, and God Himself will be among them, and He will wipe away every tear from their eyes; and their will no longer be any death; there will no longer be any mourning, or crying, or pain; the first things have passed away" Revelation 21:2-4.*

Revival is a kiss of what is to come crashing into what currently is.

It's the realized dream of every believer to truly be close to the Lord and to see His goodness in the land of the living.

But when it ends... what do you do?!

How do you respond?

Do you celebrate what just took place?

Or do you grieve that it is over?

I found myself doing both and also, frankly, a little confused and disorientated. So, I did what I do when that happens. I picked up my Bible and sat before the Lord to read, to pray and to listen. I didn't necessarily feel like I was going to encounter the Lord. Funny how faith, or lack thereof, works. I sat down in my now empty sanctuary on a weekday morning and began to read the Word.

I wasn't looking for anything. I just knew it was good for me and I knew that I could not abandon the habits and disciplines that have sustained me for years in the absence of the mighty visitation of His Spirit that just ended.

I found myself in the Gospel of John and the resurrected Jesus was on the beach speaking to His friends, the apostles.

"So when they had finished breakfast, Jesus said to Simon Peter, 'Simon, son of John, do you love Me more than these?' He said to Him, 'Yes, Lord; You know that I love You." He said to him, 'Tend My lambs.' He said to him again a second time, 'Simon, son of John, do you love Me?' He said to Him, 'Yes Lord; You know that I love You.' He said to him, 'Shepherd My sheep.' He said to him the third time, 'Simon, son of John, do you love Me?' Peter was grieved because He said to him the third time, 'Do you love Me?' And he said to Him, 'Lord, you know all things; You know that I love You.' Jesus said to him, 'Tend My sheep.' John 21:15-17.

I had read this passage many times. But this time it was different. It was as if I was there standing on the beach with them. Jesus, full of love and compassion was speaking to his apostles. And there was Peter; fireball Peter; "I'm gonna go all the way and set the world ablaze" Peter; Revivalist Peter; Zealot Peter... and Peter was me.

I could just see the Lord walk over and put His hands on either side of my face, gaze into my eyes with firm love and resolve and ask me the question: "Jeff, do you love me?".

This is not the question I'm expecting to be asked! I'm the guy that just shut down everything in the church to host a move of God!

"Of course, I love you Jesus!"

He replies, "Tend my lambs."

He goes on and asks me again, "Jeff, do you love me?"

He continues, "Then I want you to take all of that fire, and burning passion for me and for revival and for impacting the world, and I want you to show me that love by being tender with the people I send you."

And then it hits me: Even though I love Him, I may not be communicating that love to Him in the way that He is looking for.

Those of us that are married should understand this. We love our spouses and our hearts are for them, but sometimes our actions do not communicate the love that we feel internally. Often it requires us to change the way we are doing something so that the love that we feel for that individual is getting communicated in a way that can be received as love by the object of our affection.

Call it a love language if you want.

Jesus spoke to Peter and now He was speaking to me, "Do you love me? Then I want you to show me that love by tending My lambs, shepherding my sheep, feeding them, being patient with them, being nice to them. After all, they are my sheep. Take all your zeal, all your passion, all your fire and funnel that through tenderness and care for the people that I send you."

I was wrecked.

I was wrecked, and I was humbled.

Ever since I was a young man and had encountered Jesus in the back of my High School Library, I have felt this calling, this beckoning into "the deep" of God's heart. I have wanted to be a burning one... Someone who is carrying the fire of His Presence and the passion of the Gospel in a real and tangible way.

I wanted to be willing to suffer, willing to endure, and willing to walk through anything and everything that the Lord may call me to.

That attitude had served me well.

It had gotten me this far at least.

But now I am sitting with the Lord after one of the most "radical" and profound seasons of His Presence and His Power invading my life. Our entire church community had been swept up into a very real and tangible outpouring of His Spirit.

And here I am, sitting before the Lord and what does He say?

"Be tender. Be kind. Be patient. Feed my sheep."

It was like a radical baptism into the meekness of God!

It felt like God's kindness, and it felt like a rebuke.

Again, it felt like Jesus grabbing me by the side of my face, peering into my eyes and saying, "Jeff! You radical! Jeff, I need you to take all your fire, and all your passion, and all you zeal and all your love for me and I want you to express all of that to me by loving the people I send to you more deeply. Jeff, I want you to take your passion for my Gospel, and your passion for my Presence, and your passion for seeing a move of God, and I want you to be tender with the people that I send you. Be tender Jeff. I will feel the love that you have for me as you learn to be more tender with the people that I send you."

It stung. It hurt. It wounded and it healed.

It was a Father moment.

Like a father putting his arm around the son that he loves and then sharing a hard word of correction that will help his son continue to grow and mature, so too my heavenly Father was loving me with a hard word.

After a moment of great breakthrough and great blessing came a great rebuke and a great invitation to a new level of supernatural meekness and a baptism into the shepherd heart of God.

The shepherd heart of God that does not despise the weak; does not despise the broken.

The shepherd heart of God that does not look down on our frailty and does not push away the dysfunctional.

The shepherd heart of God which seeks to save and heal and restore.

The same heart that is calling your name and mine today… to draw a little closer… get a little lower…listen a little longer… and come home to the Father's house.

To the place where ambition dies.

To the place where patience grows.

To the place where comparison ceases to exist, and love rules the day.

He's calling you and He's calling me:

"Be tender to the people I send you."

"Be tender with my lambs."

Give us the grace, Lord Jesus, to respond to you well.

LETTER NINE

A HARD FALL

"Anyone who falls on this stone will be broken to pieces; anyone on whom it falls will be crushed." Matthew 21:44

"Therefore humble yourselves under the mighty hand of God, that He may exalt you at the proper time" 1 Peter 5:6

IT HAD BEEN A VERY, VERY HARD TWO YEARS.

My wife and I had moved our family to a different state in order to serve a pastor and his new church plant.

We were invited to "come and be mentored" and we felt like that was exactly what we needed in that season.

We once again sold many of our things and gave the rest away to move to outside of the D.C. beltway in order to jump in and serve our new church family.

Just over a year earlier, Jesus had called my wife and I to quit our secular work and sell our home and to "step out of the boat" and walk on water... to pursue our calling in ministry and to follow wherever Jesus would call us.

In order to work with this church plant and in order to position ourselves to be mentored, I had to go back to work in the very same vocation that I had left: the car business.

It seemed like another death… another blow.

It felt like Abraham who waited for his promised child, only to have the Lord then ask to sacrifice that same child on an altar. That altar, the altar of submission, worship, surrender, and trust, was calling my wife and I to trust the Lord with our dreams… the dreams that He Himself put in our heart!

I went back to work and through myself into the ministry. I was working 12-hour days and things were just really hard.

The recession hit in full force. I fell behind financially as no one was buying the luxury cars I was trying to sell! But I worked and worked and when I was "off" I was throwing myself into the ministry.

I was the worship pastor.

I was the prayer pastor.

I was the youth pastor.

I was the "everything else" pastor.

I would arrive at my pastor's house around 7am on Sundays, load his van with the sound equipment, arrive at the hotel where we were meeting, set up the equipment, lead worship and then break it all down after the service.

It was my "job" at the church. I am not afraid of hard work and so I threw myself into it. Week in and week out I gave it my best. I gave it my all. I wanted to see God move and I was more than willing to "pour myself out" as an offering of service to my God.

It wasn't too long after that I realized things weren't going the way we had imagined.

The church wasn't growing… at all.

It was small when we got there and it seemed to be getting smaller.

The services were "plowing times". They were generally hard and difficult to get through.

Beyond that I had moved my family to the church in order to be mentored, discipled, and developed.

Again, I wasn't looking for a handout. I was ready to work. "Put me in coach!"

But in the approximately 3 years we were there, I would probably meet with my pastor one on one around 10 times.

I didn't understand it! I was giving it everything I had! Why didn't he want to meet with me?

All my father issues and rejection issues came roaring to the surface. I felt rejected. I felt abandoned. I felt used.

Yes I had been praying "God use me!" for years. But now it was happening and I was really hurting! (Irony intended).

I was fasting. I was praying. I was working hard. I was enduring suffering and hardship and persevering. But it didn't seem to actually be "doing" much of anything. In fact, it seemed to just be the "circle around the storm". All around me was difficulty, misunderstanding and hardship.

Then one day my pastor handed me the book "The Tale of Three Kings," by Gene Edwards.

It is truly an incredible book. It tells the story of King Saul, and David, and Absalom. It calls the reader to greater humility, submission and trust. It has been a blessing in my life and continues to be so and I highly recommend everyone reading it.

But if you are ever in a situation where you are not getting along with your pastor, and there is tension, and he gives you the book, the message is "Don't be an Absalom."

You know, Absalom, the son of David (the greatest king found in the Bible and the reference point for every king who ever followed after him), who decided he would be a better king than David. He betrayed his father, usurped the throne and led a search party to kill his own father. THAT

Absalom.

In the end God would defend David, and it would be Absalom, not David who would lose his life.

The thing was, I didn't want to be an Absalom. I wasn't trying to be an Absalom. I didn't think I was an Absalom.

But I was arrogant.

I was prideful.

I was cocky.

And anointed... and sincere... and legitimate.

And a great candidate to be an Absalom... to make churches that would lead people away from the pastor and towards myself.

I remember sitting down to read the book and I read about how men draw people to themselves... men who appear to have the cleanest of intentions, and yet are wrecking balls in the end. Men who are willing to wreck and destroy another man's work in the pursuit of their own.

Who among you is wise and understanding? Let him show by his good behavior his deeds in the gentleness of wisdom. But if you have bitter jealousy and selfish ambition in your heart, do not be arrogant and so lie against the truth. This wisdom is not that which comes down from above, but is earthly, natural, demonic. For where jealousy and selfish ambition exist, there is disorder and every evil thing. But the wisdom from above is first pure, then peaceable, gentle, reasonable, full of mercy and good fruits, unwavering, without hypocrisy. And the seed whose fruit is righteousness is sown in peace by those who make peace. James 3:13-18

I read how men like Absalom never feel called to go somewhere where they don't know anyone to start a new work. They always feel called to go across town or across the street. They never ask people to follow them, but people ask them, and they reluctantly agree. In so doing they participate in a wickedly demonic spirit, clinging to their outward righteousness, unleashing destruction and tearing down what others have given their lives to build.

In that moment I put the book down and I said, "I will NEVER do that." I said, "God, if you ever want me to start a church, send me to a city where I don't know anyone.

A little time after that a friend called. I should probably say, "a mentor called," for this man was many years my senior with decades of ministry and pastoral experience. The Lord had put me on his heart, and he called to check in on me.

"Things are horrible!" I vented. And so began my laundry list of discontent. My older and wiser friend listened to me with empathy and restraint. I don't know how long I went on but after I exhausted my frustrations, my friend spoke. But he spoke, not with human wisdom, but with the wisdom that comes from above.

"For My thoughts are not your thoughts, Nor are your ways My ways," declares the LORD. For as the heavens are higher than the earth, so are My ways higher than your ways and My thoughts than your thoughts."

Isaiah 55:8-9

"The right word at the right time is like precious gold set in silver." Proverbs 25:11 CEV

And the Lord spoke through my friend in that moment:

"Humble yourself. Submit to your pastor. Restore your relationship, and then leave with a blessing."

What?!

What about my grievances? What about my pain? I've worked so hard and I've given myself in prayer and fasting and labor and toil. I've had promised made to me that were broken and I'm hurting!

"Humble yourself. Submit to your pastor. Restore your relationship, and then leave with a blessing."

One more time for effect:

"Humble yourself. Submit to your pastor. Restore your relationship, and then leave with a blessing."

I knew it was the word of the Lord.

I knew that I was accountable to walk it out.

I knew that if I did not, it would be sin.

"Therefore, to one who knows the right thing to do and does not do it, to him it is sin." James 4:17

In that moment "I determined to know nothing". I turned off my brain. I silenced my judgments. I humbled myself and began seeking to be a blessing instead of seeking to be right.

And God moved.

And His Presence came.

And tensions began to go down.

And the skepticism and distrust that had been directed towards me started to cease.

About six months would pass.

My church began to merge with another church community. My wife and I knew that the merge signaled the end of our assignment to serve our church and our pastor. We decided to take a week to fast and pray and to seek the face of God for direction for our lives.

It was during that week that I was in a prayer time on my face in my bedroom when I heard the Lord tell me to move to Lynchburg Virginia to start a new work there. It was a city in which I did not know anyone. (TECHNICALLY, I knew two college students...But they were not residents.)

I told my wife what I had heard the Lord say. Then I followed it up with "If any of these 5 pastors and mentors in our life say they do not think it is the Lord, then we won't do it."

I knew that there was power in being sent and not just going.

"How will they preach unless they are sent?" Romans 10:15

I wanted to arrive in Lynchburg with an apostolic blessing and apostolic authority for an apostolic calling.

The first person I approached to submit my plans and the word that I had received from God was my pastor. The pastor I had been serving. The pastor whom I had trouble relating to and connecting with. The pastor that was skeptical towards me and suspicious of my motives.

The pastor that I had humbled myself before, sought to make him feel sure of my love and support of him, and had won back his favor and trust.

It was that very same pastor that I submitted my word to, and it was that very same pastor that affirmed it was God and laid hands on me to bless me in my next season.

There was no vision, trance or dream. There was simply a word spoken in season by a trusted friend. A word that was spoken that called me to a lower place, a meeker place, a humbler place. It was that word that allowed me to transition from a place of great pain, to a place of great fruitfulness.

May God's word always be faithful to do the same for you.

"For You have tried us, O God;
You have refined us as silver is refined.
You brought us into the net;
You laid an oppressive burden upon our loins.
You made men ride over our heads;
We went through fire and through water,
Yet You brought us out int a place of abundance."
Psalm 66:10-12

LETTER TEN

THE JOURNEY CONTINUES

SO, WHERE DO WE GO FROM HERE?

Paul said this:

> *"I know a man in Christ who fourteen years ago – whether in the body I do not know, or out of the body I do not know, God knows – such a man was caught up to the third heaven. And I know how such a man – whether in the body or apart from the body I do not know, God knows – was caught up into Paradise and heard inexpressible words, which a man is not permitted to speak. On behalf of such a man I will boast; but on my own behalf I will not boast, except in regard to my weaknesses." 2 Corinthians 12:2-5*

Most all theologians believe Paul was speaking of himself in this passage. We know for sure that Paul was speaking of himself when he said the following:

> *"Because of the surpassing greatness of the revelations, for this reason, to keep me from exalting myself, there was given me a thorn in the flesh, a messenger of Satan to torment me – to keep me from exalting myself!"*

2 Corinthians 12:7

Incredible.

This passage doesn't fit that well into most of our modern theological boxes. It is both true that Paul was given a "thorn in the flesh, a messenger of Satan" but it is also true that he was given it "because of the surpassing greatness of the revelations."

Paul spoke to the Corinthians church elsewhere and told them, "Knowledge makes arrogant, but love edifies." 1 Corinthians 8:1.

Some of you may be familiar with the King James rendering:

"Knowledge puffeth up, but charity edifieth."

It goes on:

> *"And if any man think that he knoweth any thing, he knowing nothing yet as he ought to know. But if any man love God, the same is known of him." 1 Corinthians 8:2-3*

So what does it all mean?

Well, for starters, I hope it means that I did an adequate job sharing my failings as much as my encounters. My weaknesses (and they are many) abound. My "revelations" are much fewer and farther in between.

I've been walking with Jesus for about 20 years now. I am more acquainted today with my shortcomings and failings then I was at the beginning!

Sure, at the beginning I was desperate. I knew I was a mess. I just had no idea how big of a mess I really was! Nor did I understand that the Lord would spend the rest of my life shaving off rough edges, performing open heart surgery on me and continually calling me to walk with Him in the fiery trials of life... for one thing really:

"If any man love God..."

You see it is all for the love of God.

I started this book intent on only sharing prophetic encounters and "ectstatic" experiences that I have had in the Spirit of God. But the shortcoming in that is that some of my most intense and transformational God experiences were forged not in my prayer closet but in the battle field of life. An unsaved boss curses me out but I sense the Presence of the Lord bringing correction to my slothful heart... A trusted pastor and friend calls me out of rebellion and calls me into a heart posture of submission and honor... It's moments like these where I have heard that Lord "in a different form".

"After that, He appeared in a different form to two of them while they were walking along on their way to the country." Mark 16:12.

It looked different and sounded different than what I was familiar with, but, "did not our heart burn within us as, while he talked with us by the way"? Luke 24:32.

And so, as this book comes to an end, and the next leg of your journey and mine begins can we approach it with this context:

That we would know more of God, love Him more deeply and profoundly, regardless of what it looks like, or what we are familiar with?

I love the encounters. I love it when Jesus pulls back the veil and reveals Himself to me in a way that marks me and changes me.

But I don't worship encounters.

I worship Jesus.

And for you beloved, my greatest desire is that you would love Him more.

Our God does awesome and mighty things. He can do more than anything we can ask, think or imagine. I pray that each of you experience those sweet times in His Presence where He marks your heart with His own.

But beyond all of that I pray that you would fall more in love with your Savior, your King and your God. That a new tenderness would form in your heart for Jesus.

That you would read His word and your heart would begin to burn.

That you would respond to His Spirit and say, "Yes" to Jesus no matter the cost.

I pray that in all things and in all ways, in every season of life, for richer or poorer, in sickness and in health, that you would cling to your crucified and risen savior.

He Himself is our exceedingly great reward.

May neither trials, tribulations, persecutions or sufferings; victories, miracles, visions or dreams make us lose sight of that fact.

"Now this is eternal life: that they know you, the only true God, and Jesus Christ, whom you have sent" John 17:3.

Thanks for reading! Please add a short review on Amazon and let us know what you thought!

For booking or speaking engagements with Jeff Struss, please email info@elanipublishing.com for more information.